The Throats of Narcissus

The Throats of Narcissus

Bruce Bond

The University of Arkansas Press
Fayetteville
2001

05 04 03 02 01   5 4 3 2 1

Designer: John Coghlan

⊗ The paper used in this publication meets the minimum
requirements of the American National Standard for Permanence
of Paper for Printed Library Materials Z39.48-1984.

Library of Congress Cataloging-in-Publication Data

Bond, Bruce, 1954–
     The throats of Narcissus / Bruce Bond.
          p. cm.
          ISBN 1-55728-706-6 (pbk. : alk. paper)
     I. Title.
     PS3552.05943 T48 2001
          811' .54—dc21

                                        2001000369

for Nicki
my wife, my sphinx, my casting pool by turns

Acknowledgments

Black Warrior Review: "The Flies"
Boulevard: "Echolalia"
Brilliant Corners: "Django"
Chelsea: "Two Rivers"
Colorado Review: "Mercy," "The Throats of Narcissus"
COLUMBIA: A Journal of Literature and Art: "Babble"
Crab Orchard Review: "Coltrane's Teeth"
Denver Quarterly: "Bodhisattva"
The Iowa Review: "The Drowning"
Michigan Quarterly Review: "Bill Evans"
North American Review: "Dream Vision from the Book of
    Dogs"
The Ohio Review: "The Sirens of Los Angeles"
The Paris Review: "Cruor Dei," "Narcissus," "Art Tatum,"
    "Oval"
Ploughshares: "Art Pepper"
Poetry Northwest: "Lester Young"
River Styx: "The Chimneys," "Mandala"
TriQuarterly: "Alien Hand," "Digging Up the Briars"
Western Humanities Review: "Ascension," "Amnesia"
Witness: "1979"
The Yale Review: "Thelonious Sphere Monk"

"The Sirens of Los Angeles" appeared in *American
Diaspora: Poetry of Exile* (University of Iowa Press). "Art
Pepper" appeared in *Best Texas Writing 2* (Firewheel
Editions). "Mandala" received a *River Styx* International

Poetry Award. "Cruor Dei" appeared in *Place of Passage* (Story Line Press). Special thanks to the National Endowment for the Arts, the Texas Commission on the Arts, the Texas Institute of Letters, the Austin Writers' League, the Ragdale Foundation, and the University of North Texas for their assistance during the completion of this manuscript. Also a warm thanks to Nicki Cohen, Austin Hummell, Corey Marks, Donald Revell, Enid Shomer, and Carol Sickman-Garner.

Contents

III.

I.

Cruor Dei

As if we arrived through the blind extremes
of sleep, we opened our mouths, eyes closed,
and the priest laid on our tongues his coins
of bread, what we learned never to cross
with our teeth, never to rush, for at the heart
of each was God's nerve, burning and alive.

Then we washed it down with wine and Latin—
cruor dei, God's blood, the stuff I figured
flowed in everyone's body—what did I know—
though here was the glad horror of appetite
taking it in, and memories of other gods,
how they in their stories were torn apart,

exploding into the ten thousand things,
into the still-conscious body of names
for things, with every word a hint of blood.
It's how I picture crowning into the world—
through red water over rims of bone
into a little chaos of lights and gasping.

I like to think the blade binds as it cuts,
mother from child, that each solitude
ripens into a name for the other.
And as the mother looks down, her voice
is a braid of scar tissue between them.
It draws the child further into debt

he never resolves, not wholly, but sees
in the unlikely bodies of passersby,
in the man, say, caught on film, who keeps
bending back the car door, pulling a stranger

from a seat on fire—a birth of sorts,
though none is entirely his to repay.

It's only the trace, at best, a kindness
remade the way gods remake themselves
in our image, half-naked, their hands nailed
to some bare wall in sweltering Texas.
Their feet are vines crossing in the brick shade.
They would turn us all into mothers, grieving.

And among our children: debt and hunger.
Sometimes you feel them thinking, confiding
in the barely audible speech of twins.
In bad times they almost sound like hope.
Which they are. So many cuts, so many streams
of erotic letters welling up in the rift:

a lover says goodbye in the hazard lights
of an idling taxi, a pulse in the eye
she will never quite remember nor forget,
not completely, and to live just this side
of completion is to turn further inward
the way a key of light turns in a gaze.

So it is with my father in his illness,
railing at the bolted apartment door,
cursing his wife for locking up his wife.
Or swearing he is the doctor again
with patients enthralled in another room.
He is the complicated child, the latch

lifting on an intricate cage. He scissors us
into broken flocks of memory and wish
which are his own body tearing apart,
though it is tough to say he suffers

the knowledge, our sense of what he was
or will be. It could be kindness too:

the bony dice of days stumbling through him,
the bewildering children who hold out
their shadowy bruises, too young to know
which wounds are serious—they all seem so
early on—and which ones simply clear up
with time, going clean in their own blood.

1979

When the train arrives, as memory must arrive
in its own country, the beaten breath
of the engine collapses into Berlin station,
and a man surrenders to the current of travelers,
each rising trance on the mechanical stairs,
to the echoing concourse and iron arch,

the place where hours behind him now
open out across a moat of traffic—it's midday
after all—and the flamed edifice
of the chapel sits, its public steeple bombed through
and left for good, shamed like a boy
strapped in a chair: the indelibility of guilt

and rancor, the charred lip of the gash.
Disrepair is its own monument.
And it gets more that way, more stubborn
and unlikely, as all around it streetlife rises
in bus fumes and the scent of meat,
trains smoldering to the ravenous mouth

that will not close. When the Reich fell
the city shattered into four cities,
then two, as if some warped mitosis were going
backward, yearning for history's last
absorption, one cell gazing at the other,
sequestered in its unforgiving wall.

Swallowed through the cathedral door,
a stranger to churches let alone to the fire
that brings them down, he hears the accents thickening,
the black forest of the foreign tongue,

the air breathing him. He walks a bit,
flips through a tourist pamphlet, retracing

the impenetrable facts: the gutted ribwork,
stone face, bombed chapel of the human mouth.
He enters their language as it enters him,
the way bar smoke enters a child's parka,
and the more foreign it seems the closer
the wind that brought him here, however blind,

where the horrors of trains cool in their stalls.
Silence too has a destination,
in search of the body it might step into,
the border guard waving it through
like sky into the tattered roof,
the idea of liberty into a captive brain.

Just yesterday he took a sleeper,
waking only to show his passport,
to catch a glimpse of the boarded window
thorned in wire, falling back
into sleep; behind him now
the iron shadow of the free world.

The Sirens of Los Angeles

All summer as the blacktop softens drugged
in an ether of smog and visible heat,
you hear the car stereos beat the air,
the bass throb of vans blooming at stoplights,
a shushing window and its flash of song.

Light burns on a fender in a sluggish tide
of fenders, the whole flammable basin now
littered in the oily scraps of sparrows.
I love this city, however long I soak
in the shadows of my shirt, in the dark

plumes of riot and angry script, a wash
of syringes under the pier. It's the dark
a singer leans her mike to, saying *no*
to the world the way a child says *no*.
Palms beat their shredded wings in the sun.

They too are waiting for the earth to move.
No word for the phone-pole repairman lashed
to his mast, a song blasting in his headset,
drowning the street in solitary music.
An ambulance parts the waters of our traffic—

one life, one life, it says—and the cars
wash back to bury its path. When the sun sets,
it trails a florescence of theaters
and taillights, the fresh stupor of children
streaked in purple; there's an art to forgetting

that oceans know, swallowing the day's pill
of fire. The floodlit heads on billboards lay

their smiles over the heads before them,
wave on wave of blind eyes and giant teeth.
Every day the world is growing younger.

We could drive to the darkened crest and look back,
the city cracked open like a radio.
In the distance a living wire of sound.
Copters prick the alleys with their spotlights.
We could work our lives with wax in our ears

and fool no one: even in our sleep we hear
the echoes blossom in the throats of dogs—
or is it our own sleeping throats we hear—
each heart a bottle of blood impatient
for land and feasting, longing to be poured.

Echolalia

Late in the day's contagion
of patients, my mind consumed
in my body's problems, my difficult heart,
I see a girl on the waiting-room carpet
crouched in her invisible house.
She is fitting a red plastic hammer in the hole
a doll's head should be,

pounding a nonexistent nail
into the eye of her shoe,
and to my own quiet surprise I ask,
What's wrong? What's wrong,
she says, word for word in a colder music,
as if speaking were her way
of listening, of passing my question on.

I'm not the only one between us
lost in translation, unlocking the voice
inside the voice, each voice a doll
split from another doll's belly;
whatever I say is her tongue's gospel;
she would make herself small for me.
And since she's not my child,

I'm bound to ask again, compelled
like the lonely confessor on a bus.
We could be talking to our own bodies—
our stunned pulse, a frozen hand—
waiting for replies in pins of feeling.
Heaven knows what lies there
coiled in her ear, breaking my English

down into an ever quieter English,
if what she hears is a query
descending, a little drier on her lips,
or the wraith of answers, released:
the bucket returning with air from the bottom.
It reminds me of the malice of children,
how they mimic one another into madness,

though I know better. That night I catch
my breath in the stairwell.
With every step a fading stutter of feet.
It's a story so foreign I feel mine
pale where hers begins, with a doll
whose head pounds the daylights
into the cold bright nail of sleep—

what's wrong, what's wrong, what's wrong.
I too want a way out, to make a person
of my problems and so survive them,
my heart stronger, clearer. I want to unlock
the hole in her throat with my words in it,
and I keep going there, stair after stair,
a stranger's breath on my own tongue.

The Chimneys

After the fire the monoliths of brick
it stranded laid bare their long singed throats,
char-scented, headless, blushed in a warm black
rapture of wind and shadows, thick with soot,
each a monument to the lesser fires
we tended, to the winter nights they ate
our words and still moods, those kindling fears
we buried in their jaws. They know the art
of loss is loss, how recovery begins
its blackening work. Who could hate the slip-
knots of smoke and rancor, the sap that spits,
bitter days the only way out was in.

And now to see these homes razed to cinders
as if someone freed the dreaming animal,
let it ravage the speechless body it lulled.
Take the child who watches in cold wonder
the scattering of his father's ashes,
if only one night weeks later to dream
the lightless blaze fathers dream, those flashes
under their blind eyes, grazing the screen
and dying. There are mornings no less strange,
fiery pivots in the world machine:
he might shiver in his blanket, gaze at flames
his mother built, still puzzling out what's in
this thing—if you can call it a thing—
this light that cracks like criminals, like rain.

Oval

after De Chirico

How faceless their pathos, the ovals
of these heads, huge, smooth, hermetic
as eggs, and solemn, especially the man's
angled heavily on its neck, shelled
in sleep: his bluish and drooping fingers,

the folded tide of sleeves, the whole
human collapse dreaming, pale as stone,
while above him the muse looks down,
his body half-man, half-a-makeshift
of wooden bricks, glue, plates of iron,

the failed glimmer and scrap of a life packed
into his chest. Half-monument, yes,
though corruptible, blooming with pity,
his great disproportionate hand resting
kindly on a chair. Imagine what it is

to open your body's language
like a vacant plaza—that missing arm,
was it hacked away or merely unconceived?—
a fountain drying in the salt air.
For every night in his thin coat of meat,

the machination of his gut exposed,
he becomes more of the world than the dream
remembers, more fiercely lodged
in the stubborn wire and glass of things.
Which is not a place apart from solitude.

Far from it. And the man knows this
as the uterine child knows her way out
into a still more singular life, pressed
through the wound of another's body.
See the hole in the block of the muse's lung,

that empty gaze of public statues.
The look he gives rises like a scaffold
over the face of stones and cruel time—
a muse-in-progress—which is lucky,
that he would make an expectation of loss,

a chalk-white room of physical silence,
closed, save for the door cracked
shyly behind, a thin black seam leading . . .
forward or back—difficult to say
or know what walls face off around them,

if the world is a tireless regress of rooms,
no final exit, no curtain's hem limned
in daylight—only a maze of interiors,
each no more inward than the next . . . but then,
the very notion has grown unbearable

to the man, his skin filling with the ebb
of radio and distant cars, a woman's hand
putting a polish on the heart's shell,
flush, as shells are, with rumor,
magnificent and hopeless as the sea.

Mercy

Dear happiness, forgive me;
you are not what I make histories of,
never the word inside my words:

the bright seed on the tongue
of the parakeet, lime green and chatty.
We both know you are nonsense mostly,

contrary to belief quite flightless
on your trapeze. Here now, you could be
the red worm burning in its peach;

even as I sink my teeth the blush
is fading into memoir. So it is with any star
eaten by the plain speech of day.

And what could be more fortunate,
which is why I know so little about you,
why I cannot repeat what I loved

more than these losses taken to heart.
We grow large in memory and sleep,
fluffing the pillows of our bodies,

our broken teeth turning to money:
I dreamt of you on a bicycle in the rain.
The sky was cloudless and shiny,

and I too was burning, a windy planet
liquid at the core, palmed in rain.
Then the dream was empty,

and there was only the body brimming over
with darkness, and I woke, speechless,
mouthing the sweet dark air of the room.

Digging Up the Briars

Any stretch of rain will tell you,
the bulb is what you want, nothing less:
its spindled fist of roots and curses
so rarely where you think. Which is half
the trick: to read your entanglements,

work your way down without severing
your leads, back bent to the thunk
and spit of every blinding rock.
Once you're under you're bound to lose
what's what . . . call it the unconscious

cunning of weeds, the way their fibers
twine and strangle, so when you get there,
when you catch the ganglia with your spade,
levering the shovel handle like a jack,
it's not the weight of the prize you feel,

but some force of need woven into the nervous
system of things. For every bulb
you claim, there's one you don't—
this much you know—until your arms grow
heavy in their sockets, in that ache
suspended between accomplishment

and failure, and the sleep that takes
them over, green with greed, sending
its shoots into bedsheets below.
And crowning everything the distended
hearts of leaves, bearing you up:
more light, more light.

How far
to the little orange lamps of knowledge
in their orchard? How far to the garden
gate at the end of the world,
where you just might look back
and wonder—

no surer than before—
what lies on the other side of all
that infusion of duty and desire, all
that work you worked your life for?
The wiry scribbles in books
you gave your eyes to,

the illegible
Braille of bodies wrapped in veins,
every deep allegiance that crinkled
on its coals and burst, what are they
if not the winding script of yards
you can neither finish nor forget?

Which is why you take them to bed,
because they're hopeless and they let you,
as if you could climb into them,
into every problem's helix and through.
And now you see

whole groves of them
dripping in the merciful ropes of vines.
They are the other face of roots
startled into the sky's mirror,
blown into the erotic hand of letters
you burned,

the ones you didn't,
into the work of bodies braiding
and tearing, braiding and tearing;
and out of the ground—you can almost
smell it—the sharp green scent
of rain, ascending.

The Drowning

And when they reached the ocean shore,
  the woman turned
  to her girl and said,
see there, that is the territory between
  you and your better
  self, and the child
said, what? and the mother said, that is
  the place of all
  the buried limbs,
at which the child said, I don't understand,
  I can't quite figure . . .
  and the mother cut
the child's speech at the shoulder, saying,
  the place of your foul
  and painful birth,
and the meager waves breathed like a massive
  iron lung, once,
  the mother said,
once there was a way out of my loneliness,
  my mound of broken
  shells I called *not*
yet or *almost home* or *come back, dear one,*
  and the child said, look,
  the gulls are crying
with wonderful terror at the blue above them
  and below, like meat
  in a blue sandwich,
and the mother said, no, no, you can do so much
  better, see here,
  give me your leg,
and the child did, and off it came, waves
  raked the pebbles
  with their claws,

their foam, their pleasure, and the mother said,
        look at the blue
        wound of being so far,
so cast out of your bluer, your better self,
        look at the filth
        of the sea on fire
with day's final word, no, no, you are not
        looking, give me
        your eyeballs,
and out they came, which is when the child turned up
        to the mother, gazing
        through the graves
of her missing eyes, and a pleasure-foam skimmed
        fearlessly over
        the polished sand,
shackling the child's ankle, drawing back
        through the bubbles
        of the burrowing sandcrabs.

Dream Vision from the Book of Dogs

A man was talking to a dog
in a voice that threatened to consume
them both: but this is a metaphysical poem,
he said, not an erotic one,
at which the dog cocked its head
with a look of bewildered worship,
as if the words were all one high whistle
out of the sky, when finally
I could no longer contain myself
and said, but wait, what of the poetry
of Israel and Persia—though in truth
I hardly knew what I was saying,
and it felt a little selfish,
interrupting like that—what
of the tradition of poems for dogs
whose erotic fantasies are all about food,
like the one where god appears
as a hamburger and sayeth unto the hounds,
come, come closer my little ones
and repeat after me . . . no, wait,
ouch, please don't eat me, not here,
not now, there's more, I promise . . .

Ascension

In a film run backward, bristles of mold
shiver on an apple and swell,
then worm into the fruit's bruise
and withered skin: small mouths of rot
secrete a trail of pincers and wings
more hungry than before: ants spit
the life beneath them, the rosy head
freshly fallen, watering with white meat,
with the prospect of flight into the trees,
into the receding fuses of stems,
the starved sweet armor of the seed.

So too in my sleep: so much blighted
fruit rising in the low limbs:
I am handing my father another nail,
another mini-flagpole, up the silver ladder.
He keeps making the indoors ours,
nailing our minor nation to the earth.
Time beats its faceless hammer,
nail by nail, thrill by thrill
passing through a father's hands,
which could take both my boy hands
in one warm swallow, put a nail to bed

in a dead swoon . . . when poof,
the miss, the gash, the crushed
metal of our Father's name,
the way he crumples, glazed and moaning,
a mist flown from the river inside.
And as the blue deepens in his thumb,
the moon-crest of his cuticle
plum-blue, he could be praying

in his anger: all those invisible nails
going up, banging into the floor of heaven.

It's the sound of any number of hands
under the hammer, any son's
needy worship swelling into the fruit
of his shame: one child's domain
shatters into little countries,
into apples falling out of the sky.
To think a father's body is born
in blood into the boy's mind, his sleep
dissolving, how gods redden before
another's stare, becoming an afterlife

of stares. Just when I believe
the final motions of prayer pin a shield
at cardinal points, they turn
to the crosshairs of a distant rifle,
the treasure map x, hope's wound.
No bed of nails, not here, not
the picked scabs of children or saints,
the way boys rub their wounds together,
blood brothers fathering themselves.

Only the pain you never own,
the one that tears another man
from the tree and eats. And it keeps eating
that way, as if what little you know
of always is the teeth it has,
here, now, on the brink of another
hungry grave, with some flash
of doubt that restores to the world
a place, plunges its shovel
underground and levers up, refreshed.

II.

SOLO SESSIONS

Art Pepper

I keep seeing him as the tiny chill
of sound rising out of a black groove,
this record and its mist of scratches,

and imagine it would have pleased him,
to think he could escape this planet alive.
Or the other notion, how he is more

needle than sound, that a piece of him
lies down still: you can feel it sinking,
tapering into the music he's in.

Each phrase is a kind of vein that way,
a small bruise swelling on the vine.
Music, he said, would keep him young.

And it did. With every song a pilot
sleeping at the speed of light. True,
there were nights to survive, so many

rituals that fixed him to his body
they seemed another man's life to him:
a thin face floating in a hot spoon.

It became his memento mori, this face,
shuttling in and out of its locket,
growing thinner by the year. And always

his arrival at the same still pool,
the white translucent skin of syringes
blushing briefly in the aftermath.

In the end it was his own sweet blood
he shot, however foreign, newly tainted.
It became his second wind, a chaser.

See, you *can* cheat death, he said, leaning
into the mike (they could have been anyone
in the dark, listening) then he blew

a pip of air into his sax to clear it.
It must have sent a shiver through the crowd,
as if to play this freely took a streak

of thievery or spite—he split his lip
to prove it—so that music was a black market,
a sting, the way he winged it over bridges,

taking apart the heads of tunes in fakebooks.
What he played best and longest he closed
his eyes to hear, as if darkness made him

more permeable to sound, more absorbent,
like a black plate standing in the sun.
Death deserved him after all, having come

so near . . . at least he thrived to think so,
amazed to live so deep into the red,
to pass the loan shark of his last day,

though the future kills no one and is
nowhere and knows nothing of the moment
in the back of a cab when a bulbed vein

broke in his cortex and he looked up
at his wife's face, stung by her panic,
slowly lapsing into the numbness of her arms.

And who alive can resist the next thing,
what it was to drown in himself, rushed
from a world of strange affections? All

those heads with his saxophone in them,
at the record store, say, where a man might
flip through a bin of releases and pause

to listen, half-blinded by the sheer speed
of joy, the stillness at the heart of it,
the music welling up like blood in his brain.

Thelonious Sphere Monk

Take any solo session from the Riverside
years, those long trapped breaths of dissonance
like smoke, a holding back of fulfillment
that becomes just that, our glad and broken
contract, and you hear the great sad boulders

of chords thump into place, foundation stones
for later work, entire soaring tenements
of work. Difficult at times, the way he kept
everyone waiting, those hours he stumbled
through uncharted tunes, tape rolling, until

his stagger had a heart's precision to it,
a largesse of hands startled by choice.
Which is why, beyond the scarred edifice
of tone clusters and uneven strides, each room's
waste of cups and ashes, beyond the nights

his strings soured in a New York basement,
there's a lightness here, a compulsion
to surprise. Less an end to silence
than a yielding to its wants, to the bloom
of poverty and water inside it:

sound as the hard fruit of deprivation.
And though you see him stab at the odd key,
his finger blunted like a cigarette,
it's not rage at a world slow to forgive
or understand, not merely; not the chronic

deafness of taxis and jail clerks, the phony
drug charge that left him jobless; but more

a private joy working on its problem.
To raze and resurrect, to resurrect by razing.
There are moments he seems so thickly bound

in the black suns of his eyes, his face
bearded as a buffalo, mumbling in the shade
of a dark-felt hat. How better to inhabit
the pride of disappointment, to spark
against the corners, making a language

out of a failure to speak—though in time
failure became just that, a handful of days
he refused it all: the phone calls, his wife,
his health, his music. They block-and-tackled
his spinet through the high window of a cramped

apartment. Who was he to suffer fools,
let alone his own hands; and it came on
so swiftly: the thinning of his face
in the stream of silence. Soon his piano
too was a black chest of wire and dust.

And memory was small comfort. All his life
the giant spools of pleasure and tape flowed
in one direction: how he lived, he died,
the high gothic cathedral of his style
eroding, its stones condemned, windows boarded.

Coltrane's Teeth

No less than the quarantined
cities of god and deep sleep,
they too had their secret life,

buried in a flung shatter
of nerves and carnal wires,
in the fray and knotted script

of veins he worked his music
through; what were they after all
if not the tiny Stonehenge

of the tongue, the visible
bone at the cry's horizon?
Those midnight binges of liquor

and pie, how any tumbler
in its moment might soak up
the room, sugared with bar light—

small wonder they rotted out
like trees down to the red soil
until the shyest mordent sent

chills of pain into his jaw.
Look at the little teethmarks
of heroin and lovers,

the gods who opened their wounds
and swallowed, near everything
he hungered for long enough

and hard took him in its mouth.
That's why in those later years
especially, beneath the bronze

calm of his gaze at strangers,
under the ashes of friends
and marriages, in the black

of horns the dead had left him,
or above those warm stretched rivers
of bass, you hear an anxious

writhing, a shedding of skins.
Meditations, he called them,
prayers, though figured in the clay

of questions he never quite
straightens out, strong as he blows.
Even as his teeth stumbled

crown by crown out of the trench,
a bridgework marked their losses
like tombstones worn clean, dateless,

nameless, the ghosts of all
that dissonance flown between.
Who could have guessed it had gone

this far, to see him twisting
out his phrases with such force,
with the anguished face of sex,

resisting, eyes closed, sun-blind,
his great forehead glazed with salt?
Not the abandoned body

of the panicky or numb,
but sanctified in serum,
the opacity of grief

gripped by joy; it's what you see
in fits, in the way he bit
the thrilled wafer of his reed,

dreaming of sweets, his lips
sealed about their dark work.
The more compressed the vessel

the more he poured his lungs out,
as if he were blowing glass,
the clear ache of it, blooming.

Lester Young

Just why he flared his tenor to the side,
    head cocked, reed clamp twisted in its neck,
why he bore the bell's weight in one hand—

    hours on end he braced it there—as the other
fluttered over the low valves, his cool
    resolve flush with wind . . . no one ever knew.

Sure, there were theories: for the timbre,
    the women; as he put it, *for the birds.*
Each night his sax's bella donna floated

    over the fire of tones he would never match,
never could, however many reeds he cut;
    something in his tenor dreamt it was a flute,

lithe and buoyant, a horizon in his lips.
    And when he sank into solos, his head
heavy, bemused, you could spot the black

    stones of his eyes, gin-soaked and gleaming;
discouragement or desire, he drowned it
    in music: sluggish grains of jailtime, the silk

knots in a woman's gaze, one day's rhythm
    of Pall-Malls and minor cash going through him,
or the huge sums to young tenors who copped

    entire lines he played; even music itself,
his saxophone shushing the world-shore,
    drowned in the sea of a larger music.

With every spark that pinned a tie or cuff,
	he wrapped himself in flash like a magician's
disappearing act. Final days in a bed

	at the Alvin, high above the riff of traffic,
it took a stack of LP's to put him under . . .
		that and the wide-eyed lights of the room.

Death was a flair of embittered birds borne up
	by gravity. Who could hear him and not love
that sound, the way it lingers, how he raised

	a stamen at phrase's end? Who wouldn't eat
the lotus blooming there? With every record
	a widened pupil falling on its spindle.

Art Tatum

No stranger to the faith of eyes
asleep under the surgeon's lancet,
to time gambled with every try

that slit the foam of cataracts
where they pearled, he understood
the powers of sun to make us

loyal, what it is to shadow
twilight on the eye's horizon.
Then it came: the crumpling blow

that made desire final, the day
a neighbor blackjacked and robbed him,
flooding the blotter of his gaze.

And as the wounded eye welled up
with blindness, the other followed
blind: that night an ocular cup

of flashlight dwindled down the path
in his head, over pianos
as he saw them there, glazed in pitch.

Soon he grew into living proof
that darkness deepens the mind's ear.
It quickened what his hands were made of,

all those notes mapping the faces
of chords, touching the phantom shapes.
Finesse, yes, but not the mere lace

of fancy; more a conversation
among losses, each prick of light
dissolving in its constellation.

Once he sat by a radio,
listening to a dead friend, and played
along on the air piano.

As if his fingertips had eyes
gazing into music beneath
the music, dark, mute, buried alive.

Django

Nightfall, and summer's lemon grove
of crickets shivered in its roots:
    a child napped
        under paper lilies.

In sleep his fingers spidered over
the fiddle he played all day,
    entering the trance
        inside the trance,

then a candle tipped and rolled—
a mouse, a draft, a click like a door
    locking gently
        cruelly behind.

Soon the gypsy wagon blossomed
into flame, roof pitch crackling
    his eyelids open,
        and he flared

a blanket to break the singe
and blizzard of ash.
    Fire brushed his hand
        and crimped it,

bound the pinky to its neighbor
nerve to nerve, two carpals palled
    in a singular web.
        So close a call

he saw his limbs as borrowed,
charmed, the way they weathered

the blaze of fevers
and fainting spells,

years scorched in silver nitrate,
the chrysalis-peel of failed skin.
Not to diminish
what he found

or didn't, not to make light: pain
was what it was, a rock
in the continuous stream
and rhapsody

of blood. Nights he conjured up
the most horrible diseases
to focus the mind,
to splice

the will where it thrashed about
like a power wire downed in a storm.
Snug in its coffin
his violin slept.

Welts of fretwork surfaced
in the dark; the twin serifs
of f-holes melded.
Such hunger in his gut,

the quick of a fiddle
burning there, blurry as a bee,
so when he let
the music out

its casket, when in time
his passion turned to guitar,

it felt as flush
    as meat to bone.

He too changed shape, flitting up
the tempered ladder, head bowed
    to the wooden waves
      on his knee . . .

as if it were bliss that bit
the hand, furious as roses,
    that spooked the fiery
      disfigured wing.

Bill Evans

The night he went too deep with a needle
and the feeling drained out of his hand,
he saw his keyboard as a marriage bed,

wide as it was, where the widow hand
kept crossing sides, talking to itself:
a cloud of flesh in the ebony lacquer.

With every move, he made a music
so solitary and clear people closed
their eyes and swore there were two hands there,

that no great rift had come between them.
In his lap his fingers went cold as glass.
Not that he forgot them, not completely.

What tongue forgets the numb tooth beside it?
A certain strangeness brings them closer.
Nor was he consumed by the open grave

of his hand. But distance has its own life.
And if the art of soloing is how
the fingers leave their body and flutter back

refreshed, so it was with the whole arm
sleeping on his thigh. The music in it
kept emerging, the way a father's features

emerge in a son's—those shy turns of speech
and gesture, the transfiguring face.
When his hunger took him on winter walks

in the West End, the forces of privacy
conspired to restore him; white flags
of steam spirited out of the wet street.

From a tattered chair in a basement flat,
he listened to Scriabin records, a wash-
cloth over his eyes, coffee boiling

in its pan; rain blurred the narrow windows.
And when they cleared, if you climbed the steps
to the cracked courtyard and looked up,

through the giant well of gray apartments
you could see a small rectangle of sky,
its blue page where the world began.

Sometimes he saw it when he slept, face down
as if he too were sky, blowing a hole
of sight through the floor beneath him.

What is dissonance, he thought, if not
a seam in the body, a sweet dread.
So when you lean into the sound and through,

the mind is a pupil blooming in its eye,
descending into an unlit hallway.
Or a buried theater of eyes, glinting.

I think of him in that aging footage,
his head bowed and resting on its hinge,
a trapdoor to a deeper anonymity.

Tough to tell how strung out he must
have been, if, as he began coiled up
like a man in sickness or prayer,

he felt more wakeful or asleep. Or both.
The way he backed off from the keyboard,
holding his hands at arm's length,

they became such moody foster children,
what he longed to rescue from the damage
that he did. Still they continued

to surprise him like a story that burns
its words to see by. On a good day
who wouldn't open a vein to chance?

And what is breathing if not a dialogue
between the living and the dead?
Imagine the corpus of music he left.

Every day hundreds walk through it
the way air walks to the furthest cell
and back. It's what the blood expects.

Somewhere a woman shudders like a moth
on fire, lifts her body from its flame
to lie there, winded, flushed in the dark,

and his music turns its thin black wheel
against her past, vanishing as it goes.
Someone asked him once why the habit

of rocking his fingers on the keys
at the ends of phrases, as if he could milk
the sound that way, keeping it alive.

The difference for him was how
it changed the notes before that note,
like a coffin wavering over the grave,

sliding down through the life before it.
Which is how I think of his left hand,
the way it slipped into tiny cracks

in time, wanting in. Shadow lettering,
he called it, this ghosting of the silent
beat, this body and its hollows, pulsing.

III.

Babble

Once there was music in it.
Neither silence nor speech but the current between.

Or there in the tiny deaths
of conversation, scribbling like a fly.

Once it was the pure sport of the tongue,
an unconscious joy that slipped its language.

But now I keep seeing that bruise on his hip
like ink breeding across a blotter.

And that sound: the watery horizon
of a life that would go on for miles,

the merest phosphorescence of sense, cresting.
And no one knows why it is

he raises his arms that way, looking up,
why he falls silent when he does,

his hands his only witness
playing the sterile harp of the air.

The Throats of Narcissus

The ego, captivated with its own making, its own history . . .
lures consciousness, moment by moment, into a space that has
no frame, no limit, and therefore no body . . . it becomes
bloated on an aesthetic that camouflages seams.
—Mark F. Kuras

I.

Call it a hole in silence: the bird
in this yard with the trill of a distant phone.
A tongue's needle shuttles in its throat.
Word without end, amen.

Then the sound of kids in a yard next door,
the boy's voice singing *charge*.
And they run up against each other's death,
every one of them swooning on the lawn.

Forever late—the dead—bound up
in a traffic of flies, black sparks
of the brain's fire. Overhead, a buzzing
of wires. Someone answer the phone,

they say. *Look world, I'm swooning.*

II.

Picture Medusa, her head full of worms,
as if death were an excess
of life, a breathless canyon panorama.
Soon the air below turns to stone

you carve a face in. Your iris,
a mirror, lifts the mirror

50

from its rock, so now your every prospect
drags a lengthening path

like a father at his family tree.
The roots you draw are hands
reaching for the earth's core,
for its tiny period, *Eureka,* its atom,

and the blown sky that's buried there.

III.

Not that blood alone made him restless,
but how it pulsed on the ocean
of his pillow like a stranded flashlight.
The heart a throb of option;

waves the world turning its insides out,
lathering a white nothing at the core: *if
you want to reach me you have to go through
the hungry mouths of door after door, to meet

your evening in its drunken robes and hair
like fire, its whorish sympathies dripping
in shipwreck and pills.* And so he turned away,
though no less into shipwreck, and pill,

to swell the heavy boredom of the sea.

IV.

Then the blood woke in him as a pool
of water he just stepped out of,
and he held the pool in one hand
like a magnifying glass, when no sooner

it darkened to a wound, the dead eye
in an empty camera. And then it was
the place he baptized his children,
and they drank it up like little sponges—

such tender criminals. No matter how hard
he squeezed there was always more,
the flesh soaked in it, and so in fear
he left his body—they all did—

as if it were the whole story . . .

V.

. . . as if light shone through the tiny rips
in the world's cloth. You see in a newspaper
the girl's face that disappeared
from the sheriff's parking lot last noon,

then the long straight line
of no news, that arrowing horizon
they laid her body in. The poison darts
of flowers have put the earth to sleep.

In Auschwitz once a group of prisoners
put God on trial and found him
guilty—it took what candles
they had—as if gods and men went

to their deaths together. Like lovers.

VI.

The sins of cigarettes are hubris—
Vantage, Merit, True—as if their names were

the breath words ride before they ride.
In a film a man pulls a string

of diamonds out with his teeth, right out
of her body a trickle of stones.
Smoke goes through their pockets like money.
Then he is the bell rope rising

in her tower, her voice the weight
that grips and pulls him. In each a nameless
calling: *come see the peep hole*
in its dark confessional, be the ice

weeping in its mouth, absolved.

VII.

And when he saw the river in his eye
and fell in as if he were everything
the river lost, a sky-thing with a god-
like absence, he could not know the body

he fell into was the one he left . . .
until it came: the tremor of plates
in their cabinets, God's tanks
as they broke through the city's heart

and deeper, rolled in the eyes
of televisions into the curfewed streets.
Like children, graves dropped open their mouths,
whole choirs of them. And the bold

white shirt fluttered on his back.

Two Rivers

When my mother's mind is two contrary rivers
becoming one frightened eye of water,

she takes the long way back to sleep,
down the hall to the kitchen thermostat,

her face the color of refrigerator light.
It's been that way ever since her spine began

its tenement collapse, scrawled with anger.
With every step a spark of shabby wiring.

Soon fear became one of those habits,
like needles that calm, if only briefly.

We've had this conversation a million times,
there by the box collection at the foot

of her bed, those tiny carved cubes of night.
Their lids are so many disappointed wings.

Not to mention the flitting of medical books
from chair to chair, attendant as angels.

How her pain longs to prove itself, like a god,
alone, however strong the prayers and tablets

she swallows. It's become her life's work,
her difficult child, and we its children.

With every pill another symptom and its pill,
another article of faith. And what's a faith

without a little spite for the world,
the faith it takes to kill a god?

Amnesia

Each of us more alone than words,
more mountainous than the blizzard believes,
more resonant year by cavernous year.
My wife, my sphinx, my casting pool by turns,
who knew beneath her blushed chest
a patch of shame closed up its flower?
Who heard the library silence fall
over the basement carrels of her sex,
how it rose and settled with the leaves?
I lay my head on her belly,
close my eyes: *yes, says the lake*
cradled in her pelvis, ghosted with minnows,
yes, the mirror-tree, unrippled,
afraid, yes, the bird in the tree,
the unrippled song in the living bowl.

She is coming back, the girl who hides,
who picks at lint in a closet carpet.
The house she's in will burn down
in the stretch of years ahead.
Downstairs a prima donna sings
to coax the adder from its basket.
So sweet, the pianissimo barb and turn
like a trout lure in the morning sun.
As the poison rises so too her song:
remember the girl before the shameful thing?
A shy violin perches on its hairs.
Remember the tiny eggs of rage
hatching in the cool foundation.
Anger too has wings beneath its skin,
arias hushed for human ears:

shh, the sigh that turns from the meat plate steaming,
shh, the ghost as it drops its skirt,
shh, the leaky life raft going down.
The girl plants a black rose in a vase
beside a slab of tongue, a black tongue
inside the tongue, a brother's secret
wrapped like a pharaoh in a tomb of tongue.
The less she spoke the less she ate.
Smoke gathered in the library cellar
to buoy her heavenward, holy and starving.
The grim haven under coats in closets,
the charm of a father's palm on her brow,
the swan-white throat of the coloratura dangling
from a thread of air—all conspired to snuff
her fever, to bury what they could not know.

Who knew it would take a father's death
to raise the hand from the eye
of the wound? Look, it sees her.
A bed returns in bits and flashes
as if the floor were spitting light.
Somewhere a frightened girl
braces beneath her brother's weight,
somewhere the fisted confusion opens her
entrails and blooms; time abhors a vacuum,
and so it keeps its shadow rhythm:
how thin the bathrobe of a father's ghost,
the one he slips, how spellbound
the fire she huddles over, her arms
a lakeshore locked about her knees,
the mouth of her pelvis, gently rocking.

Alien Hand

It starts with the seizures,
the ones that grip her torso
in their fist so tight
they crumple life and limb
and so force the surgeons' cut,

that manhole cover of bone
in her head—unspeakable,
their mercy, how far
they go, severing a bridge
at the core of knowing.

And it works. The fits subside.
At times they nearly vanish,
as if what brought them on
was the shudder of one sphere
in the mirror of the other.

Which is where the hand comes in.
She's not alone. It's a story
that flares up time
to time, ever since they started
in on the central tissues.

For her it's the left,
that bitter child of a hand,
her oldest conquest,
never so unruly and alive.
As if it has eyes—that's how

she puts it—the way it grasps
at the pointless spoon or shirt,

trespassing where it will.
She could be anywhere,
at a friend's place, say,

where it seizes up on the scruff
of his dog, just holding it
there, giving it everything.
And the more she resists,
the stronger it gets,

until she wakes one night
to the ridiculous horror
grasping at her throat.
It's as if her seizures
were now its dwarf province

and the bad dream that quarters
the mind again and again,
bequeathing fits always
to some lesser part, cursing
the odd moment awake.

Soon the whole angry tangle
of nerve—each bitten word
in a history of words—
becomes a broken empire, a night
sliced at the coldest hour.

And with each cut, each cell
divided, the swelling memory
of the blade.

The Flies

In your little globes of shattered facets,
hands always miss. What's a hand
but a clumsy twenty-fingered thing,

a curse to ignite your hysterical fuse,
wings sparking, spitting light, zagging
from screen to screen, synaptic? Think

of the greedy pincers your world spins
into: terror's puny virtuoso, particle
and wave, fallout of the planet's

perpetual fission, perpetual surprise.
All our lives we watch you scribble
your mad epistles, punctuate our lampshades,

ripple our skins. Will we ever stop
slapping ourselves this way?
In siren-swoons of descending pitch,

you lower your minuscule chainsaws
through our trances. Cruel children,
I hear you in the lulls of abandoned meals.

Your eggs are the bird's caviar,
the ravenous ellipsis, clandestine periods
breeding periods. You are the pupil

flown free of its iris, the aqueous sparkle
of your thorax fierce with thirst.
Obsidian chip of the mind's arrow

sharpening down to no mind: you rub
your hands in silence, polish your eyes.
Then the sudden zipper in the air.

Dismantle your armor and what remains
but armor, platelets licked in black glue.
Together you are sputtering kernels

of petrified ash, thick pepper beneath
the sky's great hunger, impacted droppings
of angels, microsurgeons of the dead,

dizzy spell of the open wound. No sleep
for the tiny proboscis needling the sheen,
the blood that lights your hemispheric eyes.

Narcissus

Who's to say where the man ends,
the world begins, what it is
that breaks into a vanishing sweat,
a thing shored on a tide of linen?
Though this much is clear: as night
drags its intimate figures
back into the blackened current,
a magnificent loneliness
takes its place. Then he looks up
and sees his likeness astonished

into the mirror above him,
a pulse afloat in the elated room,
flat to the ceiling and pinned there.
Who wouldn't feel uneasily blessed,
to hover that way with your bed
on your back, bearing up under
the weight of heaven, made glorious
in the ruffled wingspan of your sheets?
And with a blinding adoration
to gaze down at your own nakedness,

cast out of the living skin,
impatient to descend, jealous,
as is the way with phantoms,
of every body your body touches?
You know the sensation: as if
your flesh were the drinking glass
forever chilled and gaping.
Perhaps you see your story float
in the open hands of a book,
thinking how distant the details

where they waver, how cold
and fragile in their clarity.
You are the breath flown out
of them, hovering there,
reading softly, the way a mother
reads to a child at night.
And like the child, you savor
every minute, every grief that turns
to pity, that leans to the mirror's
body to drink, becoming water.

Mandala

When first our mothers leaned out of the sky
and the black sun afloat in each iris
pressed down on us with its bright O,

who could resist the possibilities there,
wet and startled out of the body?
It could have been a photonegative

of the sun, its eclipsing twin, its sign,
and as it dipped below the mind's horizon
into the anonymous hands of scribes,

they laid it down onto sheets of music
and so found their emblem for sacred meter,
each measure a spinning trinity,

a sound whose circumference is everywhere,
whose center is the hungry mouth expanding.
And at the center of that was a name

for the unspeakable, the moon of a vowel
exhaled through its zero, clouding the loft.
It spread like a choir of yawns, a glorious

boredom, a falling into enormous sleep.
And like sleep, music was work, night's long feathering
of circles to gobble up the lives we loved.

Take any life. One day home from a friend's
funeral I did my laundry half-beat
half-charmed by the Walkman wires drooping

from my ears, killing time. And as I dozed
by the dryer's window, its mandala
in a hot spin of arms and legs, I saw

the world through a monocle of cellos,
each theme turned, entangled, turned away.
For the moment there could be no body

more unnerved more self-possessed than the man
exhumed there, as if the moments of one
life might blister into one moment

circled in hymns about the gravesite,
its skin dissolving into musical
horror. You've been here, I'm sure: everywhere

you go concentric waves of news are rippling
from the radio towers, and shamelessly
music, for all it refuses to admit,

sweetens in the worst times, withdrawn like us.
O, the opera singer bleats opening
a hole at the bottom of his problems.

O, he sings again recycling the note
like a plate at the table, like a birthday
tragedy the year remembers for us.

If you listen close, you hear the updraft
of the heart's triple beat, the way it surges
into nowhere and back; it sends a rush

into the breakable throats of bottles,
floats caskets up the sanctuary lanes
through the wings of doors, and people follow.

In the name of the Father, the Son,
and the Least Historical Spirit among them,
the anacrusis, the most like music

where it tips us out of our withered skins.
If, in the small-geared clockwork of a dead
monk's celibate dream of things, the down-

beat signified God, then the lightest was . . .
you tell me—His rest? His only daughter?—
her name a chemise over the air we speak.

When I was a boy each year more silent
at the table, mouth shushed to the chronic
fear and bicker of my household, I floated

a mobile of planets over my bed,
their names those of immortals who died
into a soundless music, a sky to sleep by.

Our Father who art in heaven, I thought
wondering why He did His art so far
away, His blood-stained fingers drafting spheres.

Mickey Mouse and Buddha, wherever you are,
what could be more reassuring to a child
than the island of a circular tummy

or head, what could leaven a body more?—
which is why you are the guardians
of so many private shrines, you who

never show us your age, who survive
in a world you're not quite of, attuned
through the radars of such perfected ears.

Once I truly believed the world was round:
every Fourth of July life began: we set fire
to another fuse and ran from the tunnel,

the hoop-shaped boom chasing after us like cops.
Once we spun our battered records, entranced,
ground them with needles and blind affection.

Walls and fathers shuddered to the sounds
we shadowed on air guitars, the broad
mirage of warm bass rising through our bodies.

It made us feel both minuscule and large,
like the dream of women the deeper the pulse
the greater our surrender, the more we wanted

to be Alvin Lee pacing the stage
at Woodstock: *I'm going home,* he sings,
then a spasm of notes over the high frets,

the animal cry of the thinnest string,
going home, he repeats, a tireless boy
in the phoenix of his volume, playing

rings around us all, until the whole wide
dervish cymbal-crashes to a thump and cheer,
and he unstraps his tattered instrument,

mounts a melon on his shirtless back
and stumbles, dire thin, sweat drenched, out
of his own brief spectacle like a god.

❖

Once there was no end to the large eyes
of breasts watching over our every move.
The sun dragged them out of me each morning,

just as it dragged April and its brush-
fire of dahlias right out of the ground.
Self-important weeds raised their snifters and chimed.

No peace for the redwing and the worm it drops
through a bristle of sticks and little throats,
in each a chirping, desperate for flight.

Soon I lost my fingers in the bright-
black current of a lover's hair, first nights
she unhooked the steel button in her jeans

and so broke the circle that divided
her body, my boyish hands faithless as pigeons.
It was the nearest thing to touching all

of her at once, this perpetual moving,
the way a tongue moves in and out of words
it shapes: O, she said, and I—no less

aloft, welling up with zeros—I would have
replied in kind, if not for the eclipse
of threshold-awe laid to the layer

of shadow between us. There I was
on the brink of each iris. Then she quickened
beneath me, like a river before a fall.

❖

I love the fluted vaults of chapel ceilings,
the lures of arcs that vein the very sky
they hide, how they magnify the shyest

cough or footstep, the quietest guitar.
They bring a body to its knees. *Anyone
there?* and the hollows reply, *there? there?*

What we pin to the tips of altar candles
are so many thinly burning signatures,
their lives distended, woven into domes.

You can feel them in the lifted sternum
of the waltz—all those paired bodies cresting,
the florescence of their near flight—and there

in the caught breath of the shrunken mother
who dreams of coming full circle, reborn,
or blowing off the great world wheel entirely.

I thought of her the night the last tornado
warning came (some local woman's voice—so
it is with warnings, the more local the more

final) the time winds cut into the map
we watched, and the TV screen went coal black
and lamplights followed, when my wife and I

and our puzzled cat huddled in the cellar,
above us the storm of God's enormous eye.
We held flashlights to the ice-green hands

of watches, so slow in their arc, sweep
after sweep to cross our small appointed time,
now and then a bluster of rain and panic,

the querulous cat claw scratching at the door,
until it was clear, silent, terror's circle
a passing over, touching nothing we knew.

I thought of the mother under the eye
that would scour her face clean off the world,
how it feels to be watched, vortex descending,

the fits of words flying like furniture.
Beneath an IV's staggered drip of serum
she listens for the pulse in uncreated

music, a blur on a piano wire.
No circle of friends or hours can still it,
no jar of lilies, however strong.

It is the needle pulling at her life's
filament, a vital line of fear and sight
drawn outward through the closing eyelet.

Bodhisattva

What coaxes flowers to Buddha's footprint
is how much they leave in staying behind.
Always the equanimity of rock,
the body it imagines plumb to earth's beam
of implosion, leaning nowhere, vapored like a trick.

What loosens buds to open in the shallow
pond of shade, to drink the clean-water prayers,
shriveling there with drink's abundance,
is a calm in the beneficent toes, ovular
as olives, washed in the pumiced hands of monks.

What guest ghost visits this slab of stone,
molded to a stamp more permanent than stone?

Devotee of no one leg, he favors none
to strike a pose or poser, to lever the other
slightly aloft. Some stillness travels light
that way, the eye tending left, right,
pulled nightward down the moving sidewalk.

Hunter, surgeon, widow, even weeds look down
through a small door in the common planet.

I dreamt once my favorite shoes were ears
pressed into the world and listening.
Somewhere a thousand hooves. A cloud of dust.
There's power to burn in any man's legs,
the deathbed we rise from, day after day.

Notes

The poem "The Throats of Narcissus" is dedicated to Austin Hummell.

The epigraph for "The Throats of Narcissus" comes from "Jung's Relevance to the Postmodern Condition," by Mark F. Kuras, *Quadrant* XXX, no. 1 (2000), 25–26.